Ripley's
Believe It or Not!®

STRANGE
COINCIDENCES

A Byron Preiss Book
A Tom Doherty Associates Book
New York

RL 4.8 IL 011-013

The Ripley's 100th Anniversary Series:

Weird Inventions and Discoveries
Odd Places
Strange Coincidences
Wild Animals
Reptiles, Lizards and Prehistoric Beasts
Great and Strange Works of Man

Ripley's Believe It or Not!
Strange Coincidences

Copyright © 1990 by Ripley Entertainment Inc.
Cover design by Dean Motter
Interior design by William Mohalley
Edited by Howard Zimmerman and Megan Miller

A TOR Book
Published by Tom Doherty Associates, Inc.
49 West 24th Street
New York, New York 10010

ISBN: 0-812-51286-3

First Tor edition:

Printed in the United States of America

0 9 8 7 6 5 4 3 2 1

INTRODUCTION

Welcome to the special Centennial Edition of "Ripley's Believe It or Not!," the most famous and best known entertainment feature in the world. The centennial series is designed to help celebrate the forthcoming hundredth anniversary of Robert L. Ripley's birth in 1993.

Ripley was one of the most fabulous and interesting personalities of the 20th century. He spent his life traveling the globe in pursuit of the odd, bizarre, and incredible-but-true stories that have filled the "Believe It or Not!" pages for over 70 years. During this period, more than 80 million people in 125 countries have been entertained and amazed by Robert L. Ripley's creation. In addition, millions more have marveled at the incredible oddities on display at the Ripley's museums in America, England, Canada, Australia, and Japan.

Ripley's amazing worldwide industry is a true American success story, for it started humbly with one man and an idea.

In 1918, the twenty-five-year-old Ripley was a hard-working sports cartoonist for the New York Globe newspaper. It happened one day that he was stuck for a cartoon to draw. As his daily deadline approached, he was still staring at a blank sheet on his drawing board when inspiration struck. Ripley dug into his files where he kept notes on all sorts of unusual sports achievements. He quickly sketched nine of the more interesting and bizarre items onto his page, and a legend was born. That first page was titled "Champs and Chumps." Ripley's editor quickly came up with a snappier name, and "Believe It or Not!" became an overnight sensation.

In 1929, Ripley published his very first collection of "Believe It or Not!" in book form. It was an immediate success. A few years later his feature was appearing in over 200 newspapers in the United States and Canada alone. But Ripley was just getting started. With financial backing from his newspaper syndicate, Ripley traveled thousands of miles in the next few years. He visited 198 countries, bringing back oddities, antiques, and amazing stories from each place he stopped. The best of these eventually wound up in his famous syndicated feature. The amazing truth is that Ripley supplied at least one "Believe It or Not!" every day for thirty years!

In 1933, Ripley collected many of his fabulous treasures and put them on exhibition in Chicago. Within a year, his "Odditorium" had hosted almost two and a half million people. They lined up around the block to see the displays of shrunken heads, postage-stamp-size paintings, treasures from the Orient, incredibly intricate matchstick models, and wickedly gleaming instruments of medieval torture.

Soon after Ripley died in 1949, his unique collection of oddities was gathered and displayed in the first permanent "Believe It or Not!" museum in St. Augustine, Florida. And, fittingly, Ripley himself became one of its more amazing items. A full-size replica of the man stood at the door, greeting all visitors and giving them a foretaste of the astonishing objects they would see inside.

Although Robert L. Ripley passed away, his work lives on. The Ripley's organization has ceaselessly provided daily "Believe It or Not!" pages through the decades, always reaching a bit farther for those fantastic (but true) stories that stretch the imagination. And they are still actively seeking more. If you know of any amazing oddity, write it down and send it in to:

Ripley's Believe It or Not!
90 Eglinton Avenue East, Suite 510
Toronto, Canada
M4P 2Y3

There are now over 110,000 "Believe It or Not!" cartoons that have been printed in over 300 categories. These include everything from amazing animals to catastrophes to "Strange Coincidences," the volume you hold right now. So sit back, get comfortable, and prepare to be astonished, surprised, amazed, and delighted. Believe it or not!

THE **U-35** A GERMAN SUBMARINE
ESCAPED A DIRECT HIT BY A
BRITISH TORPEDO IN THE ATLANTIC
WHEN THE PROJECTILE SUDDENLY
HURTLED OVER THE SUB-- *MERELY
DAMAGING ITS GUARD RAIL* (1915)

HARRY BOWDEN

of Durham, England,
*WAS STRUCK TWICE
BY LIGHTNING!*
In 1968 a rake was torn
from his hands and in
1969 a bolt ripped his
slacks to shreds, tore
off his jacket, burned
off the bottom of his
socks and split
his shoes —
*YET HE ESCAPED
WITH MINOR BURNS!*

THE TRAGEDIAN WHO COULD NOT ESCAPE TRAGEDY

AESCHYLUS (525-456 B.C.) AUTHOR OF 70 GREEK TRAGEDIES, NEVER WENT OUTDOORS DURING STORMS BECAUSE AN ORACLE HAD WARNED HIM HE WOULD DIE BY *A BLOW FROM HEAVEN* —

SITTING OUTDOORS IN GELA, SICILY, ON A SUNNY DAY, HE WAS KILLED WHEN AN EAGLE MISTOOK HIS BALD HEAD FOR A ROCK AND *DROPPED A HUGE TORTOISE* ON HIM TO BREAK ITS SHELL

IN THE 1920s, A HORSE NAMED "LUCKY WONDER" USED A TYPEWRITER TO SPELL OUT ITS PSYCHIC PREDICTIONS INCLUDING THE RE-ELECTION OF PRESIDENT TRUMAN and THE U.S. ENTERING WWII!

A **NEEDLE** EMBEDDED IN THE KNEE OF MRS. **HELEN JENSEN**

Seattle, Wash.

WHEN SHE WAS A SMALL CHILD — WAS **REMOVED** FROM HER **BABY-30** YRS. LATER

THE MAN WHO COULDN'T BE HANGED

JOSEPH SAMUELS, SENTENCED TO DEATH FOR BURGLARY IN HOBART TOWN, AUSTRALIA WAS GRANTED A REPRIEVE BY THE GOVERNOR AFTER *THE ROPE BROKE 3 TIMES* (1803)

RALPH and CAROLYN **CUMMINS** of Clintwood, Va., ARE THE PARENTS OF 5 SINGLY-BORN CHILDREN-- *EACH BEING BORN ON A FEBRUARY 20th*

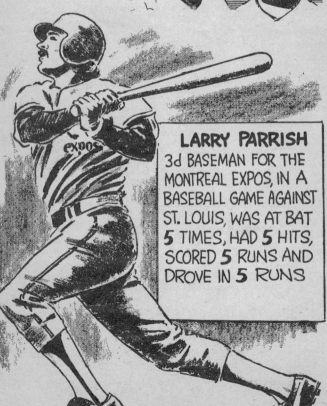

LARRY PARRISH 3d BASEMAN FOR THE MONTREAL EXPOS, IN A BASEBALL GAME AGAINST ST. LOUIS, WAS AT BAT **5** TIMES, HAD **5** HITS, SCORED **5** RUNS AND DROVE IN **5** RUNS

MABEL MARIE HUGHES ROEBUCK (1901-1984) of West Newton, Pa., IN 1901 WAS BORN ON *THANKSGIVING DAY,* IN 1919 MARRIED ON *THANKSGIVING DAY* AND IN 1984 DIED ON *THANKSGIVING DAY !*

LINDA KEEN and LINDA KEAN
of Sumter, S.C.   of Columbia, S.C.
ASSIGNED TO THE SAME ROOM AT
THE UNIV. OF SOUTH CAROLINA PURELY
BY COINCIDENCE, ARE THE SAME
HEIGHT, BOTH HAVE LONG BLONDE HAIR,
WEAR THE SAME SIZE SHOES AND
RINGS, EACH HAS A BROTHER AND A
SISTER, BOTH ARE DAUGHTERS OF
RETIRED COLONELS AND BOTH DRIVE
THE SAME MODEL CAR

ALL 12 EGGS
IN A CARTON PURCHASED
BY BETTY AND MARVIN MARX
OF SILVER SPRINGS, MD.,
HAD DOUBLE YOLKS

THE BULLET THAT FOUND ITS MARK AFTER 20 YRS!

IN 1893 HENRY ZIEGLAND, Honey Grove, Tex. JILTED HIS SWEETHEART WHO KILLED HERSELF. HER BROTHER TRIED TO AVENGE HER BY SHOOTING ZIEGLAND BUT THE BULLET ONLY GRAZED HIS FACE AND BURIED ITSELF IN A TREE. THE BROTHER, THINKING HE HAD KILLED ZIEGLAND, COMMITTED SUICIDE.

IN 1913, ZIEGLAND WAS CUTTING DOWN THE TREE WITH THE BULLET IN IT — IT WAS A TOUGH JOB SO HE USED DYNAMITE AND

THE EXPLOSION SENT THE OLD BULLET THRU ZIEGLAND'S HEAD—KILLING HIM

MRS. RUDOLPH BROWN
of Lawrence, N.Y.
BECAME THE MOTHER OF TWINS ON *MARCH 4,* 1958
HER MOTHER BECAME THE MOTHER OF TWINS ON *MARCH 4,* 1935
HER SISTER BECAME THE MOTHER OF TWINS ON *MARCH 4,* 1949

THE HOTELS THAT COLLIDED ON A HIGHWAY

THE SPRINGWATER HOTEL, A 3-STORY STRUCTURE IN WENATCHEE, WASH., WASHED OFF ITS FOUNDATION BY A FLASH FLOOD, *CROSSED A 60-FOOT-WIDE HIGHWAY AND COLLIDED WITH THE TERMINAL HOTEL* (Sept. 5, 1925)

SHERIFF HENRY PLUMMER
OF BANNACK, MONTANA,
WHO WAS FOUND TO BE MOON-
LIGHTING AS A HIGHWAYMAN,
WAS HANGED ON A GALLOWS
HE HAD BUILT HIMSELF
FOR THE EXECUTION OF
A HORSE THIEF

THE SHIP THAT FOUND ITS WAY HOME!

The **DORA**, A WHALER FROM PORT TOWNSEND, WASHINGTON, CONVERTED INTO A STEAMER BY THE ALASKA STEAMSHIP LINES, LOST HER ANCHOR AT COLD BAY, ALASKA, DRIFTED WITHOUT POWER OR COMPASS AND *ENDED UP 92 DAYS LATER AT HER OLD HOME PORT IN WASHINGTON* HAULED OUT OF THE WATER, SHE WAS FOUND TO HAVE MADE THE VOYAGE WITH HER HULL STOVE IN--KEPT AFLOAT ONLY BY A ROCK IMBEDDED IN THE GAPING HOLE

CHECK AND DOUBLE CHECK
A BANK CUSTOMER WHO TRIED TO CASH A CHECK IN MONROE TOWN- SHIP, N.J., WAS ARRESTED WHEN THE TELLER TURNED OUT TO BE THE LINDA BRANDIMATO TO WHOM THE *CHECK WAS MADE OUT*

THE PAINTING ITS SUBJECT VALUED MORE THAN LIFE!

LORD NELSON FASCINATED BY WEST'S PAINTING OF "THE DEATH OF WOLFE" AND FLATTERED BY THE ARTIST'S PROMISE TO PAINT HIM IN THE SAME MANNER, SAID:

"THEN I HOPE TO DIE IN THE NEXT BATTLE!"

LORD NELSON WAS KILLED IN HIS NEXT BATTLE—AND THE ARTIST KEPT HIS PLEDGE

THE **SHIP** THAT COULD NOT ESCAPE ITS FATE

THE "PRISCILLA" WHICH SANK OFF HUON ISLAND, TASMANIA, WAS RAISED AFTER 6 YEARS AT THE BOTTOM OF THE SEA AND PUT BACK IN SERVICE --*BUT WAS WRECKED AGAIN NEAR THE SPOT WHERE IT HAD CAPSIZED 31 YEARS BEFORE*

IDENTICAL TWINS

MARK NEWMAN AND JERRY LEVEY, ADOPTED BY DIFFERENT FAMILIES FIVE DAYS AFTER THEIR BIRTH, IN 1954, DID NOT MEET AGAIN UNTIL 1986— 32 YEARS LATER ... BOTH ARE VOL- UNTEER NEW JERSEY FIREMEN AND A FRIEND SPOTTED THEIR RESEMBLANCE AT A FIREFIGHTERS' CONVENTION

THE MAN WHO WAS CLEARED OF A MURDER CHARGE BY A CLASSIFIED AD

Jesse Boorn
of Manchester, Vt.,
WHO WAS CONVICTED OF
MURDERING HIS BROTHER-IN-LAW,
RUSSEL COLVIN, WAS FREED
WHEN AN AD IN THE RUTLAND
HERALD ON NOVEMBER 29, 1819
RESULTED IN THE DISCOVERY
*THAT THE SUPPOSEDLY SLAIN
MAN WAS ALIVE AND
LIVING IN DOVER, N.J.*

IN 1990, IN PATAN, INDIA, TWO HINDU BRIDES MARRIED THE **WRONG MEN** IN A DOUBLE WEDDING, DUE TO THE BRIDES' HEAVY VEILS, BUT THE MARRIAGES WERE DECLARED *FINAL* BY VILLAGE ELDERS!

MEL COHEN of Gravois Mills, Mo., LOST A GOLD MEZUZAH, A RELIGIOUS SYMBOL, WHILE CLEANING FISH ON HIS DOCK *AND FOUND IT 5 MONTHS LATER INSIDE A BASS HE CAUGHT WHILE TROLLING*

THE MAN WHO WAS SAVED BY A RAILROAD WRECK!

JERRY SIMPSON, WORKING ON A BRIDGE IN THE CASCADE RANGE, WASHINGTON, SAW A RUNAWAY NORTH PACIFIC ENGINE BEARING DOWN ON HIM, AND PREFERRING INSTANT DEATH TO CRIPPLING INJURY *THREW HIMSELF ACROSS ONE OF THE RAILS*

THE CAREENING ENGINE'S WHEELS ROSE FROM THE RAIL A MOMENT BEFORE HE WOULD HAVE BEEN KILLED—*AND THE ENGINE CLEARED HIS BODY AND CRASHED INTO THE GULLY BELOW* (1886)

BLASI HOFFMAN (1765-1843)
A RICH MISER of Borken, Germany,
LOCKED HIS MONEY IN A
SAFE IN HIS ROOM EVERY
NIGHT AND SLEPT WITH THE
KEY UNDER HIS PILLOW—
AT THE MOMENT HE DIED ON
THE NIGHT OF JULY 9, 1843
THE SAFE DOOR FLEW OPEN !

WHEN THE PILGRIMS LANDED IN 1620
THEY WERE GREETED BY AN INDIAN
WHO SPOKE ENGLISH !

———

IN 1614 CAPT. THOMAS HUNT RAIDED THE COAST
OF NEW ENGLAND AND CARRIED OFF 20 INDIANS
WHOM HE SOLD AS SLAVES IN SPAIN— EXCEPT
ONE WHO WAS SMUGGLED BACK TO NEWFOUNDLAND
AND FINALLY RESTORED TO THE MASSACHUSETTS
TRIBE BEFORE THE PILGRIMS ARRIVED.

GEORGE CLARK CHEEVER
of Warsaw, Ind.,
MARRIED
RACHEL ANN HASE ..
3 OF HIS SONS BY
A PRIOR MARRIAGE
ALL MARRIED SISTERS
OF **RACHEL HASE** .. AND
HIS DAUGHTER, ANNA,
MARRIED **SAMUEL HASE,**
A BROTHER OF RACHEL

BORN TO BE TOGETHER

MR. AND MRS. CHIP STALTER MARRIED ON MAR. 11, 1985, IN HILLSDALE, N.J., WERE **BOTH BORN ON THE SAME DAY,** OCT. 21, 1959, **IN THE SAME HOSPITAL AND THEIR MOTHERS EVEN SHARED THE SAME ROOM**

A STRANGE REUNION

WORLD WAR II VETERANS DANLEY SCHIEBEL AND JOHN RELIC WERE REUNITED IN 1984 IN A KANSAS CITY, KANS., HOSPITAL --43 YEARS AFTER BEING INDUCTED INTO THE ARMY ON THE **SAME** DAY-- BOTH ALSO ENTERED THE HOSPITAL ON THE **SAME** DAY, RECEIVED THE **SAME** ROOM, HAD THE **SAME** PHYSICIAN, THE **SAME** HIP OPERATION -- AND BOTH LEFT ON THE **SAME** DAY... ONLY THEIR BILLS WERE *NOT THE SAME!*

ABRAHAM
LINCOLN

WAS THE 2nd MEMBER
OF HIS FAMILY TO DIE
BY AN ASSASSIN'S BULLET

THE OTHER WAS
HIS GRANDFATHER

BOTH VICTIMS WERE NAMED ABRAHAM
BOTH HAD A WIFE NAMED MARY
BOTH HAD A SON NAMED THOMAS

THE **ST. CHARLES HOTEL**
IN NEW ORLEANS, WAS
DESTROYED BY FIRE IN 1851--
AS WAS A SECOND HOTEL
OF THE SAME NAME,
ON THE SAME LOCATION,
43 YEARS LATER

THE **BLACKTHORN
TREE** at Bra,
Italy, HAS BURST
INTO BLOOM ON
THE COLDEST
DAY OF WINTER
ANNUALLY FOR
**639
YEARS**

BELIEVE IT OR NOT!
ANGEL SANTANA, OF
NEW YORK CITY, ESCAPED
UNHARMED WHEN A
ROBBER'S BULLET *BOUNCED*
OFF HIS PANTS *ZIPPER!*

A **CRUISER** HURLED ONTO THE BEACH AT Westport Point, Mass., IN THE NEW ENGLAND HURRICANE OF 1954, WAS NAMED *"LAST FLING"*

THE GENERAL WHO SAVED HIS LIFE BY BUYING THE WRONG-SIZED HAT!

GENERAL HENRY HETH (1825-1888) LEADING A CONFEDERATE DIVISION IN THE BATTLE OF GETTYSBURG, WAS HIT IN THE HEAD BY A UNION BULLET BUT HIS LIFE WAS SAVED BECAUSE HE WAS WEARING A HAT 2 SIZES TOO LARGE - WITH NEWSPAPER FOLDED INSIDE THE SWEATBAND THE PAPER DEFLECTED THE BULLET AND THE GENERAL, UNCONSCIOUS FOR 30 HOURS, RECOVERED AND LIVED ANOTHER 25 YEARS

JOHN
JAMES
AUDUBON
(1785-1851)
THE NOTED BIRD ILLUSTRATOR
WAS ONCE SO DEEPLY IN DEBT
THAT HIS CREDITORS TOOK
EVERYTHING HE OWNED-- EXCEPT
*HIS BIRD PICTURES, WHICH
THEY CONSIDERED WORTHLESS*

CHARLES LAMB RACING EDITOR OF THE BALTIMORE NEWS AMERICAN, *PICKED THE WINNERS OF ALL 10 RACES AT DELAWARE PARK* - July 28, 1974 -

SNOW

fell 3 times in New England in 1816 in July—fulfilling a prediction in that year's edition of the Old Farmer's Almanac— *INSERTED AS A PRINTER'S PRANK*

BIRDIES THE HARD WAY! WILLIAM PINE AND OSCAR W. CARLSON PLAYING IN A FOURSOME AT LAGUNA HILLS GOLF CLUB, CA., CHIPPED SIMULTANEOUSLY AT THE 12th HOLE, THE BALLS COLLIDED -- AND BOTH DROPPED INTO THE CUP

A **BRIEFCASE** CONTAINING $5,000 WORTH OF BONDS REGISTERED IN THE NAME OF **PAUL DEVRIES** OF SAN FRANCISCO, CALIF. WAS FOUND ON A GOLF COURSE BY **PAUL DEVRIES** OF DALY CITY, CALIF. *THEY ARE NOT RELATED AND NEVER MET*

THE DAY IT SNOWED ON THE SAHARA

SNOW FELL ON GARGAFF AND SERIR BENAFFEN IN THE MOST ARID SECTION OF THE SAHARA ON JAN. 6, 1913, TO A DEPTH OF 4 INCHES -*THE AREA'S ONLY SNOWFALL IN 3,000 YEARS*

THE PEACE POPLAR

PLANTED IN JENA, GERMANY, IN 1815, TO CELEBRATE THE END OF THE NAPOLEONIC WAR WITH FRANCE, TOPPLED SUDDENLY 99 YEARS LATER ON AUGUST 1, 1914 --THE START OF WORLD WAR I

KATY JACKSON and **ESTHER COTTON**
SISTERS, 76 AND 56 YEARS OF AGE,
LIVED FOR 10 YEARS IN ROSEBURG, ORE.,
A CITY OF 14,000·· **WITHOUT KNOWING
THEY WERE SISTERS** (1961-1971)

CHRIS WHITE, 16,
and **CHRIS YERBY**, 18,
ADOPTED BY
DIFFERENT
FAMILIES, WERE
ENROLLED IN THE
SAME CORPUS
CHRISTI, TEXAS,
HIGH SCHOOL,
BECAME GOOD
FRIENDS AND
EVENTUALLY
DISCOVERED
*THEY WERE
BROTHERS* !

2 HEARTS BEATING AS ONE

FLORENCE GRAZIANO OF CHICAGO, HOSPITALIZED WITH A MINOR HEART ATTACK, VISITED HER MORTALLY ILL HUSBAND SALVATORE IN HIS ROOM AND THEN RETURNED TO HER OWN ROOM AT THE ILLINOIS MASONIC HOSPITAL... *AT THE EXACT MOMENT HE DIED ON JULY 30, 1984, HER HEART STOPPED BEATING!*

HOW TO STAY YOUNG—
ELIZABETH ELCHLINGER OF PARMA, OHIO, AND HER SON MICHAEL WERE BOTH BORN ON FEB 29, WHICH COMES ONLY ONCE EVERY FOUR YEARS! THE ODDS OF A MOTHER AND SON BEING BORN ON THAT DATE ARE OVER 2,000,000 TO ONE

H.L. MENCKEN (1880-1956) THE AMERICAN EDITOR AND CRITIC, MET THE WOMAN HE MARRIED WHEN HE GAVE A LECTURE ENTITLED, *"HOW TO CATCH HUSBANDS"*

In 1978, DOUG PRITCHARD, AGE 13, OF LENOIR, N.C., WENT TO HIS DOCTOR WITH A SORE FOOT. HE FOUND A TOOTH GROWING IN THE BOTTOM OF HIS *INSTEP*!

ON APRIL 1990, AS GHAR AHANI OF IRAN WAS KILLED WHEN A SNAKE COILED AROUND HIS RIFLE AND **SQUEEZED** AGAINST THE TRIGGER!

SIR **THOMAS BRISBANE** (1773-1860) WHO SERVED IN THE BRITISH ARMY FOR **70** YEARS DIED IN THE BED IN WHICH HE WAS BORN — *YET IN HIS* **87** *YEARS HE HAD SLEPT IN IT ONLY TWICE* **ONCE ON THE DAY HE WAS BORN AND AGAIN ON THE DAY HE DIED**

THE COAT THAT HAD A TRAGIC PATTERN OF DEATH
JABEZ SPICER of Leyden, Mass.
KILLED BY 2 BULLETS ON JAN. 25, 1787, IN SHAYS'
REBELLION AT SPRINGFIELD ARSENAL, WAS WEARING
THE COAT IN WHICH HIS BROTHER DANIEL HAD BEEN
SLAIN BY 2 BULLETS ON MARCH 5, 1784
*THE BULLETS THAT KILLED JABEZ PASSED THROUGH
THE SAME 2 HOLES IN THE CLOAK THAT HAD BEEN
MADE WHEN DANIEL WAS SLAIN 3 YEARS EARLIER*

SAN DIEGO
IN 1916 HIRED RAINMAKER CHARLES MALLORY HATFIELD TO FILL ITS DROUGHT-STRICKEN RESERVOIRS ··· OVER 15 INCHES OF RAIN THEN FELL CAUSING BILLIONS OF GALLONS OF WATER TO INUNDATE THE CITY! WHEN HATFIELD DEMANDED HIS $10,000 FEE, THE CITY FATHERS O.K.'D IT -- PROVIDED HE PAY $3,500,000 IN DAMAGE SUITS FILED AGAINST THE CITY

A POCKET GUIDE TO NEW YORK CITY, ISSUED IN **1864**, WAS FOUND BY GERMAN SUAREZ OF MEDELLÍN, COLUMBIA, MORE THAN A CENTURY LATER *IN THE BRAZILIAN JUNGLE*

WALTER BRENNAN
THE FILM ACTOR, DID NOT
BECOME SUCCESSFUL UNTIL AS
A YOUNG MAN MOST OF HIS
TEETH WERE KNOCKED OUT IN
A MOVIE FIGHT AND HE FOUND
*THAT WITHOUT THEM HE
COULD PLAY ROLES
AS AN OLD MAN*

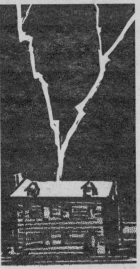

ROBERT CLIVE (1725-1774) THE BRITISH SOLDIER AND STATESMAN TWICE WAS SAVED FROM SUICIDE AS A YOUNG MAN WHEN HIS PISTOL MISFIRED *--BUT AFTER ACQUIRING FAME AND FORTUNE, KILLED HIMSELF IN HIS THIRD ATTEMPT AT 49*

LIGHTNING STRUCK THE HOUSE OF R. SCOTT ANDRES OF VIRGIN ARM, NEWFOUNDLAND, CANADA, ON JULY 4, 1985-- THE VERY NEXT NIGHT ON JULY 5TH, HIS SISTER'S HOUSE IN NORTH BAY, ONT., *WAS ALSO STRUCK BY LIGHTNING !*

THE **OPERA STAR**
WHO GOT HIS INITIAL VOICE
TRAINING AS A PEDDLER
ÉTIENNE LAINÉ (1747- 1822)
A VEGETABLE PEDDLER IN PARIS, FRANCE,
CAME TO THE ATTENTION OF THE
DIRECTOR OF THE ROYAL ACADEMY
OF MUSIC IN 1774 WHEN HIS
SHOUTS OF "BUY MY ASPARAGUS"
SHATTERED A WINDOW
IN THE DIRECTOR'S OFFICE
THE PEDDLER BECAME A STAR
TENOR FOR THE PARIS OPERA

SHE GETS "CREDIT" FOR CATCHING A THIEF DIANE KLOS, CASHIER IN AN IRVINGTON, N.J., STORE, WAS GIVEN HER OWN STOLEN CREDIT CARD FOR A PURCHASE BY A CUSTOMER WHO CLAIMED TO BE HER! DIANE AND HER BOSS CHASED THE THIEF FROM THE STORE AND SHE WAS CAUGHT BY TWO POLICEMEN

MR. and MRS. **ALBERT F. BRILES** of Cedar Rapids, Iowa, DRIVING TO A CONVENTION IN NEW ORLEANS, HAD THEIR NEW STATION WAGON STOLEN 18 HOURS AFTER THEY BOUGHT IT -- BUT THE VEHICLE WAS RECOVERED AND *THEY WON A SECOND STATION WAGON IN A DRAWING AT THE CONVENTION*

SCREEEEEEE

IN *BERMUDA* *BROTHERS,* ERSKINE L. EBBIN and *NEVILLE EBBIN* BOTH *DIED* ONE YEAR APART AFTER BEING STRUCK BY THE SAME TAXI DRIVEN BY THE SAME DRIVER AND CARRYING THE SAME *PASSENGER!*

MS **D.K. JUSTICE** *and*   **D.K. JUSTICE**
LIVES AT   LIVES AT
302½ MAPLE ST.   302½ MAPLE ST.
IN ATLANTIC, IA.   IN HUBBARD, IA.
THEY ARE NOT RELATED IN ANY WAY..

A **PEDAL ORGAN** BLOWN FROM A HOME IN GEORGIA IN 1932 BY A TORNADO, WAS FOUND MILES AWAY **VIRTUALLY UNDAMAGED**

THE MAN WHO WAS DEAD
FOR 3 DAYS!
SAI BABA
(1856-1918) of Shirdi, India,
WAS PRONOUNCED DEAD IN 1886,
WITH BOTH CIRCULATION AND
BREATHING STOPPED COMPLETELY.
AS PREPARATIONS FOR HIS
FUNERAL WERE BEING MADE **3**
DAYS LATER, IT WAS OBSERVED
THAT HE WAS BREATHING--*AND*
HE LIVED ANOTHER 32 YEARS

Mr. & Mrs JOSEPH MEYERBERG
of Brooklyn, N.Y.,
DISCOVERED AFTER THEIR MARRIAGE
THAT HER SOCIAL SECURITY NUM-
BER WAS 064-01-8089
AND HIS WAS
064-01-8090

MARJORIE and
JOSEPH WIERSZCHALEK

of Malden, Mass., married in 1959, were too broke to claim their wedding pictures — yet in April 1983, Joseph, working with a demolition crew tearing down the photographer's building, found his wedding photos in a closet *24 YEARS AFTER THEY WERE TAKEN!*

THE MONARCH WHO COULDN'T ESCAPE HIS FATE

EMPEROR ANASTASIUS I of Byzance
WARNED THAT HE WOULD BE KILLED BY
LIGHTNING, ALWAYS SOUGHT SHELTER
DURING ELECTRICAL STORMS— YET A CEILING
COLLAPSED AND CRUSHED HIM TO DEATH
*WHILE HE COWERED IN AN OLD
HOUSE DURING A THUNDERSTORM*
(518)

RALPH RIGDON ON A FISHING TRIP FROM MYSTIC, CT., LOST HIS WORKER IDENTIFICATION BADGE IN 30 FEET OF WATER OFF THE SHORE OFF FISHER'S ISLAND IN LONG ISLAND SOUND-- *AND HOOKED IT IN THE SAME SPOT TWO MONTHS LATER*

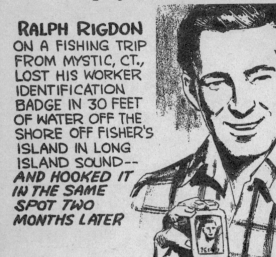

THE LUCKIEST MAN IN ALL HISTORY!

MUZAFAR JANG, A REBEL LEADER, ORDERED EXECUTED BY NASSARJANG, RULER OF DECCAN, INDIA, *WAS ABOUT TO BE BLOWN TO BITS BY A CANNON WHEN A MESSENGER RODE UP WITH NEWS THAT NASSARJANG HAD DIED!* THE MESSENGER ALSO REVEALED THAT THE REBEL, STILL TIED TO THE MOUTH OF THE CANNON, HAD BEEN ELECTED TO BE *NASSARJANG'S SUCCESSOR AS RULER OF 35,000,000 PEOPLE* (DEC. 4, 1750)

ICE HOUSE

Olson McClintock Ice House, Blanca, Colo.

BURNED TO THE **GROUND** WITHOUT **MELTING** THE **ICE** IN **IT**! (THE FIRE BURNED **2** HOURS)

THIS MOUNTAIN OF ICE THEN STOOD UNPROTECTED IN THE **SUMMER** SUN FOR **2½** MONTHS UNTIL A NEW HOUSE WAS BUILT OVER IT **60% OF THE ICE WAS SAVED!**

A BRITISH OBSERVATION PLANE
on the Western front, in World War I,
FLEW IN WIDE CIRCLES FOR SEVERAL HOURS
AND THEN LANDED WITHOUT MISHAP
*-ALTHOUGH ITS PILOT AND OBSERVER
WERE BOTH DEAD!*   June 18, 1918

THE STRANGEST JINX IN ALL HISTORY
THE "JO DAVIESS"

A MISSISSIPPI RIVER PACKET, *SANK AFTER ONLY 3 TRIPS-*
ITS ENGINES THEN WERE INSTALLED ON THE STEAMBOAT "REINDEER."
WHICH SANK AFTER 4 TRIPS-- ON THE "REINDEER II," *WHICH
ALSO SANK AFTER 4 TRIPS--* ON THE "COLONEL CLAY," *WHICH
SANK AFTER 2 TRIPS* AND ON THE "S.S. MONROE," *WHICH WAS
DESTROYED BY FIRE-* THE ENGINES WERE THEN INSTALLED IN A GRIST
MILL IN ELIZABETHTOWN, Pa.- *WHICH BURNED TO THE GROUND*

THE BABE IN THE TREETOP

A CYCLONE THAT SWEPT THROUGH MARSHFIELD, MO., LEFT AN INFANT GIRL SLEEPING PEACEFULLY IN THE BRANCHES OF A TALL ELM.

THE CHILD WAS NEVER IDENTIFIED, AND LATER WAS ADOPTED BY A LOCAL FAMILY

(April 18, 1880)

BOB PRENOSIL OF CEDAR RAPIDS, MICH., REPORTED HIS 1937 FORD TUDOR STOLEN IN 1961, AND FOUND IT AT A SWAP MEET **30 YEARS LATER!**

FRANKLIN D. ROOSEVELT

AT THE AGE OF FOUR WAS TAKEN TO THE WHITE HOUSE BY HIS FATHER AND MET GROVER CLEVELAND, TWICE PRESIDENT OF THE U.S., *BUT IN NON-CONSECUTIVE TERMS..* CLEVELAND ADVISED THE YOUNGSTER NEVER TO BE PRESIDENT, BUT ROOSEVELT GREW UP TO BECOME AMERICA'S CHIEF EXECUTIVE FOR *4 CONSECUTIVE TERMS*

A **LOGGING TRUCK**
CAUGHT IN A LUMBERMILL FIRE ON TRASK MOUNTAIN, OREGON, WAS ALMOST COMPLETELY DESTROYED, YET AFTER THE FIRE ITS TANK WAS FOUND *–STILL NEARLY FULL OF GASOLINE* (August 2, 1933)

LOTTERY LUCK STRIKES TWICE!

BILL GREEN OF THE BRONX, N.Y., IN JULY, 1984 PICKED THE WINNING NUMBERS IN HIS STATE'S LOTTERY WHEN THE PRIZE WAS $20,000,000 —BUT BECAUSE OF THE LONG LINES DIDN'T REGISTER HIS TICKET... IN OCTOBER, HE AGAIN SELECTED THE WINNERS, REGISTERED HIS TICKET AND COLLECTED $1,600,000

DEAN HAASE of North Platte, Nebr. BROKE HIS LEFT LEG SKATING ON LAKE MAHONEY ON NEW YEAR'S DAY, 1954 *HIS WIFE ALSO BROKE HER LEFT LEG SKATING ON THE SAME LAKE ON NEW YEAR'S DAY, 1955*

DETECTIVE MELVIN G. LOBBETT of Buffalo, N.Y., SHOT BY A .38 CALIBER REVOLVER AT CLOSE RANGE, WAS SAVED WHEN THE BULLET HIT HIS BADGE WHICH HE HAD DROPPED INTO HIS COAT POCKET *ONLY A MOMENT BEFORE THE SHOOTING*

A BOTTLE

TOSSED INTO THE SEA OFF THE GAMBIAN COAST
OF WEST AFRICA AND WASHED ASHORE ON
FOWL BAY BEACH, ST. PHILIP, BARBADOS
--3,000 MILES AWAY AND 8 MONTHS LATER--
BORE THE NAME AND ADDRESS OF
DAVID LAWSON KERR, *OF STIRLING, SCOTLAND.*
IT WAS FOUND ON A BEACH OWNED BY
DAVID LAWSON OF BETHESDA, Md.

A BOTTLE OF NERVE PILLS
SWEPT OUT OF THE BEDROOM
OF MRS. LENA McCOVEY WHEN A
FLOOD DESTROYED HER HOME
ON THE KLAMATH RIVER
*WAS FOUND 200 MILES AWAY
AT COOS BAY, OREGON, BY*
MRS. McCOVEY'S SISTER

PATRICK DONNELLY OF BELFAST, IRELAND, FOUND ON A ROAD NEAR HIS HOME A WALLET CONTAINING A DRIVING LICENSE ISSUED TO **PATRICK DONNELLY**— *THE WALLET WAS RETURNED TO ITS OWNER WHO WAS NO RELATION TO THE FINDER*

STANLEY CALEB McKEE of Orange, Tex., WAS BORN ON THE MORNING OF JAN. 1, 1981 --THE FIRST BABY OF THE YEAR IN HIS COMMUNITY-- AND HIS FATHER, KEITH McKEE, WAS BORN ON JAN. 1, 1955 -- *THE FIRST BABY OF THAT YEAR IN THE COMMUNITY*

STRANGE FORECAST OF GENERAL MACARTHUR'S TRIUMPH "Banzai," A BOOK WRITTEN BY GERMAN NOVELIST FERDINAND H. GRAUTOFF IN 1908, DESCRIBED A JAPANESE-AMERICAN WAR IN WHICH UNPREPARED AMERICAN TROOPS LED BY A "GENERAL MAC-ARTHUR" WERE DE-FEATED--*AND HOW THE FICTIONAL MACARTHUR RALLIED HIS MEN AND DEFEATED THE JAPANESE*

STUART CARTER A GRADUATING SENIOR AT ROSEBURG, ORE., HIGH SCHOOL SCHEDULED TO RECEIVE A SPECIAL AWARD FOR PERFECT ATTENDANCE *WAS ABSENT ON THE DAY THE HONORS WERE GIVEN OUT*

THE **TWINS** WHOSE NAMES WERE DICTATED BY NATURE!

THE MEUDELLE TWINS
WERE BORN IN PARIS, FRANCE, IN 1901
*WITH THE INITIALS OF THE MATERNAL GRANDPARENT
AFTER WHOM EACH WAS NAMED, IN THE FORM
OF BIRTHMARKS ON THEIR SHOULDERS*

THE BOY BORE THE INITIALS "T.R." AND
WAS NAMED FOR HIS GRANDFATHER,
THEODORE RODOLPHE

HIS SISTER WAS BORN WITH THE INITIALS
"B.V." AND WAS NAMED FOR HER GRANDMOTHER,
BERTHE-VIOLETTE

LYNDON BAINES JOHNSON
(1908-1973) 36th U.S. PRESIDENT,
WAS THE FIRST CHIEF EXECUTIVE
FROM THE SOUTH SINCE ANDREW
JOHNSON (17th) AND **BOTH**
SUCCEEDED ASSASSINATED
PRESIDENTS—KENNEDY
AND LINCOLN

THE PROPHECY THAT FRIGHTENED A MAN TO DEATH

CARDINAL THOMAS WOLSEY (1475-1530) WARNED BY A FORTUNE-TELLER THAT KINGSTON WOULD MARK THE END OF HIS LIFE, AVOIDED THE TOWN OF THAT NAME FOR YEARS, *BUT WHEN KING HENRY VIII SENT A CONSTABLE NAMED KINGSTON AFTER WOLSEY, HE DIED OF SHOCK*

MRS. ANNA HARAHUESS

of Coaldale, Pa., on her 77th birthday in November 1982, received birthday cards from three grandchildren, one posted in Boston, Mass., a second from Honolulu and the third from Falls Church, Va. — and all three had by chance sent *THE IDENTICAL CARD!*

HAPPY, HAPPY, HAPPY BIRTHDAY! MR. AND MRS. E.H. BISCH'S 3 CHILDREN OF SANTA ROSA, CALIF., ALL HAVE THE SAME BIRTHDAY! PEGGY, BORN MAY 28, 1954 — SCOTT, BORN MAY 28, 1958 — KRISTINE, BORN MAY 28, 1951... THE ODDS AGAINST 3 CHILDREN IN THE SAME FAMILY BEING BORN ON THE SAME DATE ARE 28,000,000 TO 1

DIEGO QUIROGA, a Spanish aristocrat, WHO HAD BECOME SEPARATED FROM HIS WIFE WHILE FLEEING MADRID DURING THE FRENCH INVASION OF 1811, HEARD A NEWBORN INFANT WHIMPERING IN A SNOW-COVERED FIELD

HE WRAPPED THE BABY GIRL IN A BLANKET AND CARRIED HER ON HIS HORSE TO THE VILLAGE OF VENTA DE PINAR – WHERE HE LEARNED THE INFANT WAS HIS OWN DAUGHTER, BORN TO MRS. QUIROGA ONLY A FEW HOURS EARLIER AND ABANDONED BY A NURSEMAID IN THE CONFUSION OF FLIGHT! THE INFANT SUFFERED NO ILL EFFECTS – AND LIVED TO THE AGE OF 80!

DON'T DRINK AND RUN

A HORSE SCRATCHED
(NOT FIT TO RUN) IN THE
9TH RACE AT BELMONT PARK
RACETRACK IN QUEENS, N.Y.,
ON JULY 11, 1985, WAS NAMED
"TOO MUCH TO DRINK"

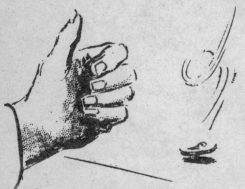

A **TOSSED COIN**
TO FALL HEADS 50 TIMES IN
A ROW, WOULD REQUIRE
1,000,000 MEN TOSSING 10
COINS A MINUTE AND 40
HOURS A WEEK--AND THEN IT
WOULD OCCUR ONLY ONCE
IN EVERY 9 CENTURIES

THE **MAN** WHO CHALLENGED FATE
-- AND LOST!

MOSES CARLTON,
A SHIP MAGNATE OF WISCASSET, MAINE,
IN 1800 THREW HIS GOLD RING INTO
THE SHEEPSCOT RIVER AND BOASTED:
"There is as much chance of my dying
a poor man as there is of ever finding
that ring again"

ONLY A FEW DAYS LATER, CARLTON FOUND
HIS RING IN A FISH SERVED AT HIS TABLE
--AND WHEN PRESIDENT MADISON EMBARGOED
AMERICAN SHIPS BECAUSE OF THE BRITISH
IMPRESSMENT OF AMERICAN SEAMEN
CARLTON DIED A POOR MAN

AFTER HER MARRIAGE IN 1924, JUDIT JACOBSTAM OF MOJA, SWEDEN, LOST HER WEDDING RING IN A HAYFIELD — IT WAS FOUND BURIED UNDER A LILAC BUSH 65 YEARS LATER!

A FISHY TALE

A MID-AIR COLLISION BETWEEN A FISH AND A JET LINER IN JUNEAU, ALASKA, DELAYED THE PLANE'S FLIGHT FOR AN HOUR... THE FISH WAS DROPPED BY AN EAGLE FLYING ABOVE THE JET

A U.S. ARMY CANTEEN CUP
WITH HIS NAME SCRATCHED ON IT,
WAS LOST BY BILL LINSCOTT OF
ADAMS, MASS., WHEN HE WAS
WOUNDED IN ITALY IN 1945.
IT WAS FOUND AND RETURNED
TO HIM WHEN HE TOURED ITALY
WITH HIS ARMY BUDDIES IN
1985--40 YEARS LATER!

DONALD CASE AND HIS STEPFATHER, GLENN McGRAW WERE BOTH STRICKEN WITH APPENDICITIS IN THEIR HOME IN ORLANDO, FLORIDA *ON THE SAME DAY !*

PAULINE E. TAYLOR and **PAULINE TAYLOR** of Detroit, Michigan, WERE BORN WITHIN 2 HOURS OF EACH OTHER AS ALMOST IDENTICAL LOOK-ALIKES AND DEVELOPED THE SAME TASTES IN DRESS, FOOD, CLOTHES AND HOBBIES, *--YET WERE IN NO WAY RELATED*

TWO TOO MANY

ROBERT ARTHUR SMITH AND ROBERT ALLAN SMITH OF CALIFORNIA AND ROBERT ANTHONY SMITH OF ILLINOIS — ALL WITH THE SAME FIRST AND LAST NAME AND MIDDLE INITIAL, AND ALL BORN ON THE SAME DAY — WERE ALL GIVEN THE **SAME SOCIAL SECURITY NUMBER—** 557-33-3757

THE
TRAGIC
TRIP
OF THE
TRUNK
THAT
DELIVERED
A BRIDES
TROUSSEAU

THE SCHOONER "SUSAN AND ELIZA"
WAS WRECKED IN A STORM OFF CAPE
ANN, MASS., AS IT WAS CARRYING SUSAN
HICHBORN—ONE OF ITS OWNER'S DAUGHTERS—
TO HER WEDDING IN BOSTON

ALL 33 PERSONS ON BOARD PERISHED, AND
NO TRACE OF THE SHIP WAS EVER FOUND
—EXCEPT FOR A TRUNK BEARING SUSAN'S
INITIALS AND CONTAINING HER TROUSSEAU
WHICH WAS CAST ASHORE AT THE
FEET OF HER WAITING FIANCÉ!

THE VERMONT STATE FAIR HELD IN WHITE RIVER
JUNCTION, VT., WAS PLAGUED BY RAIN THE
ENTIRE WEEK ANNUALLY FOR 30 YEARS
THE OPENING DATE WAS CHANGED REPEATEDLY
IN AN ATTEMPT TO GET GOOD WEATHER—BUT
IN 1928 THE FAIR WAS ABANDONED

THE SON WHO FOLLOWED IN HIS FATHER'S FOOTSTEPS — *TO THE GRAVE!*

BARON RODEMIRE de TARAZONE of France WAS SLAIN IN 1872 BY AN ASSASSIN NAMED CLAUDE VOLBONNE, AND 21 YEARS EARLIER HIS FATHER ALSO WAS MURDERED BY A CLAUDE VOLBONNE — *YET THE TWO ASSASSINS WERE NOT RELATED!*

R.I.OGLESBY of Joshua Tree, Ca.,
CASTING IN LAKE CAHILLA, CA.,
CAUGHT A TROUT BY HOOKING A
LEADER ATTACHED TO ANOTHER
HOOK IMBEDDED IN THE
FISH'S MOUTH (Nov. 26, 1975)

A GREEN PARROT
OWNED BY THE PROPRIETOR
OF A N.Y. CITY RESTAURANT
AND BAR WHO WAS MURDERED
ON JULY 12, 1942, *IDENTIFIED*
THE KILLER! THE BIRD HAD
BEEN TAUGHT TO IDENTIFY PATRONS
BY NAME AND *KEPT REPEATING*
THE NAME OF THE MURDERER!

DWIGHT D.
EISENHOWER
WHO BECAME ONE OF THE MOST
SUCCESSFUL COMMANDERS IN HISTORY,
WAS ADMITTED TO WEST POINT,
IN 1911, ONLY BECAUSE THE AP-
PLICANT WHO RANKED AHEAD
OF HIM IN HIS ENTRY TEST
FLUNKED THE PHYSICAL

**THE ODDS --
15 TRILLION TO ONE!**
EVELYN MARIE ADAMS OF POINT PLEASANT, N.J., WON HER STATE'S PICK-6 GAME TWICE, COLLECTING $3.9 MILLION IN 1985 AND $1.5 MILLION IN 1986! BETWEEN HER TWO BIG PRIZES, SHE WON $500 IN THE LOTTERY'S DAILY GAME

A ONE DOLLAR BILL
INSCRIBED WITH HIS NAME, WAS SENT BY ELLEN RICE OF BORGER, TEX., IN FEB. 1984, TO HER GREAT-GRANDSON JAMES H. GREEN IN OKLAHOMA CITY, OKLA.··· HE SPENT IT AND IN JUNE THE SAME BILL WAS TENDERED AT A CONCESSION STAND *OPERATED BY MRS. RICE IN TEXAS*

THE JEST THAT PROVED PROPHETIC !

EDWARD MOORE (1712-1757)
THE ENGLISH DRAMATIST,
ALTHOUGH APPARENTLY IN
PERFECT HEALTH, SENT
HIS OWN OBITUARY TO THE
NEWSPAPERS ON **FEB. 27, 1757**
-*GIVING THE NEXT DAY
AS HIS DATE OF DEATH*
HE SUDDENLY BECAME ILL
-AND DIED ON **FEB. 28, 1757**

HENRY BALDWIN (1780-1844) A JUSTICE OF THE U.S. SUPREME COURT, INVOLVED IN A DUEL AS A YOUTH, ESCAPED DEATH ONLY BECAUSE HIS OPPONENT'S BULLET *LODGED IN A SILVER DOLLAR IN A POCKET IN FRONT OF HIS HEART*

THE **MONARCHS** WHO **LOOKED LIKE IDENTICAL TWINS** CZAR NICHOLAS II of Russia AND **GEORGE, THE PRINCE OF WALES,** WHO LATER BECAME KING GEORGE V of England, *DELIGHTED IN PASSING THEMSELVES OFF AS EACH OTHER WHEN THE CZAR VISITED ENGLAND IN 1893*

GEORGE ROMAN OF LAUSANNE, SWITZERLAND, CONVICTED OF 30 *ROBBERIES* AND SENTENCED TO 3 YEARS IN PRISON, WAS IDENTIFIED BY *EAR MARKS* HE LEFT ON THE DOORS OF HOMES HE ROBBED.

LISA GREENE

of Miami Beach, Fla.,
was born on April 1,
1956, which was
**APRIL FOOLS' DAY,
EASTER SUNDAY
AND PASSOVER**

BIRD BRAIN WINS A MINT
BY DROPPING WOODEN CHIPS
WITH THE RIGHT NUMBERS
FROM HIS CAGE, "ROSCOE,"
A PARROT OWNED BY CARL
AND GEORGEANN SAWYER
OF OCEANSIDE, CALIF.,
SELECTED FIVE OF SIX
WINNING LOTTO NUMBERS
ENABLING THE COUPLE TO
COLLECT $ 257,525

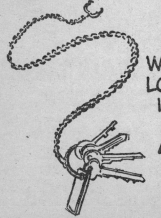

A KEY CHAIN
WITH SEVERAL KEYS
LOST BY C. DORNQWAST
IN THE WOLF RIVER
OF WISCONSIN
**WAS RECOVERED A
YEAR LATER IN A
6-LB. "WALL EYE"
PIKE**

JAMES JARVIS OF STRATFORD, ONT., CANADA, RECEIVED A $47,000 *PIANO* AS A GIFT FOR ANSWERING A NOTE HE FOUND *INSIDE A BOTTLE!*

TWO SISTERS

— Lisa Batters, 24, Carrie Borland, 22 — and Lisa's
sister-in-law, Donna Rowe, 28, all gave birth to
babies at the Royal Victoria Hospital of Barrie,
Ont., Canada, by natural means
WITHIN 6½ HOURS ON THE SAME DAY!

EMMETT and KARL
KELLY   WALLENDA

THE FAMED CLOWN AND THE RENOWNED
AERIALIST, BOTH OF WHOM HAD STARRED
IN THE RINGLING BROS. AND BARNUM AND
BAILEY CIRCUS IN NEW YORK, BOTH
DIED ON THE DAY THAT CIRCUS
OPENED IN NEW YORK— *WALLENDA
ON MARCH 22, 1978 AND KELLY ON
MARCH 28, 1979*

JUDGE JAMES BARLOW AND JUDGE JOHN BENAVIDES

TOTAL STRANGERS--WERE EACH MARRIED IN SAN ANTONIO, TEXAS, ON DEC. 22, 1951, BOTH HONEYMOONED IN MONTERREY, MEXICO *-AND THE WIFE OF EACH MAN GAVE BIRTH TO A DAUGHTER ON THE SAME DAY-- JAN. 11, 1953 -- IN THE SAME HOSPITAL-* BOTH MEN ARE NOW DISTRICT JUDGES IN SAN ANTONIO AND BOTH HAVE COURTROOMS ON THE 2ND FLOOR OF THE BEXAR COUNTY COURTHOUSE

THE HUMAN CORK!

CASIMIR POLEMUS of Ploërmel, France,
WAS INVOLVED IN 3 SHIPWRECKS
- AND EACH TIME WAS THE SOLE SURVIVOR!
HE WAS THE SOLE SURVIVOR OF THE "JEANNE
CATHERINE," WRECKED OFF BREST ON JULY 11, 1875,
THE "TROIS FRÈRES," WRECKED IN THE BAY OF
BISCAY ON SEPT. 4, 1880, AND "L'ODEON," WRECKED
OFF NEWFOUNDLAND ON JAN. 1, 1882

STUART B. GRAYSON of Springfield, N. J.
WAS BORN **APRIL 4**, 1927
HIS SISTER, RHODA, WAS BORN **APRIL 4,** 1922;
HIS WIFE, HELEN, WAS BORN **APRIL 4,** 1932;
THEIR FIRST CHILD, JAN, WAS BORN **APRIL 4,** 1956

THE COMPOSER WHO WAS SAVED BY AN APPARITION CHRISTOPH GLUCK (1714-1787) THE GERMAN COMPOSER WHO REFUSED TO SLEEP IN HIS ROOM AFTER SEEING AN APPARITION OF HIMSELF ENTER IT, FOUND THE NEXT MORNING THAT THE CEILING HAD COLLAPSED ON HIS BED AND WOULD HAVE KILLED HIM

3 BOMBS

THROWN AT THE
CARRIAGE OF
EMPEROR NAPOLEON III
of France
*KILLED OR WOUNDED
EVERY ONE OF THE
156 MEN IN HIS
HONOR GUARD—YET
THE EMPEROR AND HIS
EMPRESS ESCAPED
HARM* (Jan. 14, 1858)

BOBBY WALTHOUR, A
MARATHON BICYCLE
RACER, WAS *TWICE*
PRONOUNCED DEAD
DURING A 60-DAY
RACE—BUT HE
RECOVERED EACH
TIME AND
CONTINUED TO
COMPETE!

STEPHEN LAW of Markham,
Ont. HUNTING FOR A RING
LOST BY HIS FATHER IN **5** FEET
OF WATER IN MUSKOKA LAKE
FOUND A TOPAZ RING LOST BY HIS
GRANDMOTHER *41 YEARS BEFORE*

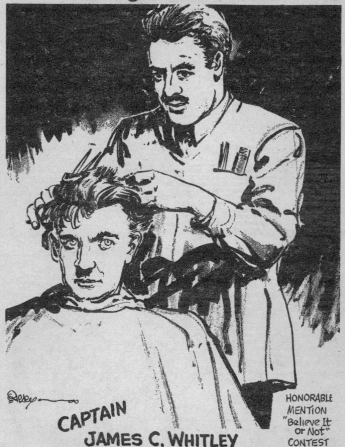

CAPTAIN JAMES C. WHITLEY

NOSE GUNNER - 15 TH AIR FORCE, Italy

WHILE CONVALESCING IN A HOSPITAL IN ITALY WAS SHAVED BY AN ITALIAN BARBER WHO HAD BEEN AN AVIATOR. *DURING THE CONVERSATION WHITLEY DISCOVERED THAT THE BARBER WAS THE SAME AVIATOR WHOSE PLANE HE HAD SHOT DOWN IN COMBAT !*

EVELYN PAGE, AN 8½ MONTH PREGNANT WOMAN FROM MEMPHIS, TN, WAS SHOT IN THE ABDOMEN *AND* SURVIVED! SHE LATER GAVE BIRTH TO A HEALTHY BABY GIRL, *BORN WITH A BULLET IN HER CHEST!*

THE DEAD MAN WHO POINTED TO HIS KILLER!
JAMES DOHERTY of Leitrim, Ireland, CONFRONTED BY A CORONER WITH THE CORPSE OF PATRICK COLIN WHOM HE WAS SUSPECTED OF HAVING SHOT TO DEATH, BROKE DOWN AND CONFESSED THE CRIME WHEN THE VICTIM'S ARM SUDDENLY ROSE AND POINTED AT THE ACCUSED MAN!
RIGOR MORTIS HAD CAUSED THE HAND TO RISE (1900)

LUCK OF THE IRISH

THE FIVE CHILDREN OF MR. AND MRS. PAUL EARLY OF SALEM, W.VA., STEPHEN, MICHELLE, JIM, CINDY AND CHERI, FOUND A SIX-LEAF, 65 FOUR-LEAF AND 20 FIVE-LEAF CLOVERS IN AN AREA OF ONLY ONE SQUARE YARD

THE **MAN** WHO FORETOLD HIS OWN DOOM TO THE HOUR!
GEORGE THALER of Gnadenwald, Austria,
PREDICTED IN 1643 THAT HE WOULD DIE
5 YEARS LATER AT 4 A.M. ON SEPT. 4th
HE DIED OF NATURAL CAUSES AT 4 A.M. ON SEPT. 4, 1648 --
AND HIS PROPHECY IS INSCRIBED ON HIS TOMBSTONE

THE **CHRISTMAS EVE ACCIDENT THAT GAVE THE VICTIM GOOD HEALTH!**

FREDERICK DAVID BURDETT A 71-YEAR-OLD GOLD PROSPECTOR IN MINDANAO, P.I., WHO SUFFERED A DISLOCATED VERTEBRA IN A 50-FOOT FALL IN 1935, WAS RUN OVER BY A HEAVY OXCART A FEW MONTHS LATER ON CHRISTMAS EVE.

HE WAS ABLE TO WALK ONLY WITH GREAT PAIN AFTER THE FIRST ACCIDENT, BUT THE SECOND MISHAP CURED HIS DISLOCATION —— *AND HE NEVER AGAIN SUFFERED EVEN A BACKACHE!*

A **STATUE** of Tlaloc, the Mexican rain god, WAS MOVED TO THE NEW ARCHEOLOGICAL MUSEUM IN MEXICO CITY IN 1964 IN THE DRY SEASON--*YET ON THAT DAY THERE WAS A TORRENTIAL RAIN*

THE **MOST BIZARRE ACCIDENT IN ALL HISTORY**

FRANCESCO delle BARCHE, VENETIAN INVENTOR OF A CATAPULT THAT COULD HURL A 3,000-POUND MISSILE, BECAME ENTANGLED IN THE WAR MACHINE DURING THE SIEGE OF ZARA, DALMATIA, *AND WAS HIMSELF HURTLED INTO THE CENTER OF THE BELEAGUERED TOWN*

HIS BODY STRUCK HIS OWN WIFE, WHO HAD ENTERED ZARA WITHOUT HER HUSBAND'S KNOWLEDGE -AND BOTH WERE KILLED! (1346)

A **PRICELESS PAINTING**
MADE OF HIS WIFE IN 1439,
BY FLEMISH ARTIST
JAN VAN EYCK,
WAS DISCOVERED IN 1808,
IN A FISH MARKET IN
BRUGES, BELGIUM, BEING
USED AS A TRAY ON WHICH
TO DISPLAY FISH

IN NICOSIA, CYPRUS, AN OMANI WOMAN WHO WAS BEING PREPARED FOR BURIAL WAS *REVIVED* AFTER HER SON, FOLLOWING TRADITIONAL MOSLEM FUNERAL RITES, SPLASHED HER WITH WATER!

IDENTICAL LICENSE PLATES ISSUED TO STANLEY GOLUCKI, OF CHICAGO, ILL., FOR 1971 AND 1972 *ENTIRELY BY COINCIDENCE*

THE **LIONS CLUB**
of Nevada, Iowa,
IN A DRAWING
FOR DOOR PRIZES
SUCCESSIVELY CALLED
ON THE REV. JAMES
DENDLER, HENRY SCUDDER,
AND WILLIAM DIAL TO
DRAW THE WINNING
STUBS-- *AND EACH*
CAME UP WITH HIS
OWN NUMBER

IN 1942, LIEUTENANT, I.M. CHISOV, A RUSSIAN PILOT, *FELL* 21,980 FT. FROM HIS FIGHTER PLANE — AND SURVIVED!

The STRANGE PROPHECY THAT FINALLY CAME TRUE

DIOCLETIAN (245-313)
TOLD BY A DRUID THAT HE WOULD BECOME EMPEROR BY KILLING A WILD BOAR — BECAME A FAMED HUNTER AND KILLED MANY A WILD BOAR — BUT IN 284 HE STABBED TO DEATH THE ASSASSIN OF EMPEROR NUMERIANUS — AND BECAME EMPEROR OF ROME!
THE MAN HE KILLED WAS NAMED APER — THE LATIN WORD FOR "WILD BOAR"

THE TOMBSTONE PORTRAIT
— Springplace, Ga.

A FEW YEARS AFTER THE
DEATH OF SMITH TREADWELL
AN EXACT LIKENESS OF HIM
APPEARED ON HIS
GRAVESTONE

PRIZE WINNER
National
Believe It or Not
Contest

THE SHARK THAT STARVED WITH A MOUTHFUL OF FISH

A FLOATING BARREL LODGED IN THE SHARK'S THROAT *WHEN THE SHARK WAS FOUND DEAD – THE BARREL WAS FULL OF FISH*

Jamaica – 1884

BROTHERS MEET HUNTING EACH OTHER'S GRAVE

GRANT AND KARL WINEGAR Marines – HADN'T SEEN EACH OTHER FOR 20 MONTHS – BUT KNEW THAT EACH WAS IN THE PACIFIC AREA. WHEN FIGHTING ON IWO JIMA – EACH THINKING THAT THE OTHER MIGHT HAVE BEEN KILLED — WENT PROWLING THRU A CEMETERY READING THE INSCRIPTIONS ON THE GRAVE MARKERS – WHEN SUDDENLY THEY MET FACE TO FACE!

Honorable Mention
Believe It or Not
Contest
TO
AURENE POUSMA,
Denver, Colo.

Mrs. MAGGIE JACOBS
of St. Joseph, Mo., FOUND
HER GREAT-GRANDDAUGHTER'S
RING, WHICH HAD BEEN LOST
FOR 6 YEARS, WHEN SHE
DISCOVERED 2 RADISHES IN
HER GARDEN HAD GROWN
TOGETHER--WITH THE RING
ENCIRCLING THEM !

CARL A. WALDMAN OF READING, PA., WAS HIT BY A TRUCK AT THE CORNER OF 11th AND SPRING STREETS, READING *--AT THE SAME TIME AS HIS SON, MICHAEL, 11, WAS INJURED BY A CAR AT THE CORNER OF 10th AND SPRING STREETS-* THEY WERE TAKEN TO THE SAME HOSPITAL AT THE SAME MOMENT -- BUT NEITHER WAS SERIOUSLY HURT

MEL GIBSON

movie actor, born in America, won his leading role in the 1979 Australian film ''Mad Max'' because the part demanded someone who looked weary, beaten-up and scarred — and Gibson had been *ATTACKED BY THREE DRUNKS JUST THE NIGHT BEFORE HIS SCHEDULED SCREEN TEST*

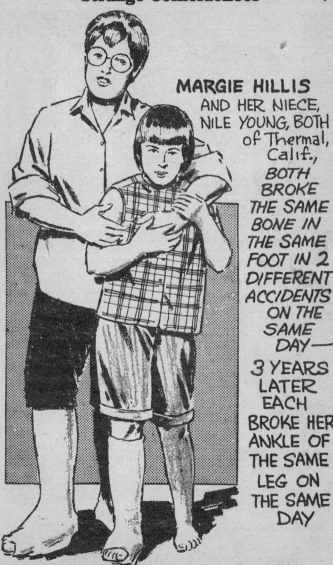

MARGIE HILLIS AND HER NIECE, NILE YOUNG, BOTH of Thermal, Calif., *BOTH BROKE THE SAME BONE IN THE SAME FOOT IN 2 DIFFERENT ACCIDENTS ON THE SAME DAY—*

3 YEARS LATER EACH BROKE HER ANKLE OF THE SAME LEG ON THE SAME DAY

THE **CATASTROPHE** THAT OCCURRED 6 TIMES ON THE SAME DATE!

SEVERE EARTHQUAKES DEVASTATED JAPANESE CITIES
ON *SEPTEMBER 1, 827*
SEPTEMBER 1, 859
SEPTEMBER 1, 867
SEPTEMBER 1, 1185
SEPTEMBER 1, 1649
AND *SEPTEMBER 1, 1923*

ON SEPTEMBER 1, 1923, TOKYO AND YOKOHAMA WERE LEVELED BY THE GREATEST EARTHQUAKE IN JAPAN'S HISTORY -WITH A LOSS OF 143,000 LIVES!

THE CORPSE THAT FOUND ITS WAY HOME
ANNE GOURLAY, A PASSENGER ON THE SCHOONER "CLAIRE CLARENDON" WHEN IT WAS WRECKED OFF THE ISLE OF WIGHT IN 1836, WAS DROWNED, BUT HER BODY WAS CARRIED 50 MILES BY THE TIDES -AND DEPOSITED ON THE BEACH IN FRONT OF HER FATHER'S COTTAGE

FRED J. SIMON OF LINCOLN, ILL., MADE A SLIDE FOR A BOLO TIE FROM TWO 30-CALIBER BULLETS -- ONE OF WHICH PIERCED THE OTHER IN THE AIR

AN **ANTIQUE CLOCK** OWNED BY MRS. MARY O'CONNOR, OF LANCASTER, CALIF., THAT HAD NOT WORKED FOR MONTHS, WAS STARTED AGAIN ON FEB. 9, 1971 BY *THE CALIFORNIA EARTHQUAKE*

THE **MAN** WHO BORE A CHARMED LIFE!

FRANK TOWER AN OILER, SWAM AWAY FROM 3 MAJOR SEA DISASTERS — THE TITANIC, IN 1912 THE EMPRESS OF IRELAND, IN 1914 AND THE LUSITANIA IN 1915

CHRISTOPHER MOEDERL

of Rosenheim, Germany, CLIMBING A FENCE ON HIS WAY TO TAKE HIS RIFLE TO A GUNSMITH FOR REPAIR, SLIPPED, ACCIDENTALLY DISCHARGED THE WEAPON, *AND WITH A SINGLE SHOT KILLED 2 FOXES*

AN **OBELISK**
ERECTED BY THE
FRENCH HISTORIAN, RAYNAL,
ON THE ISLAND OF ALSTAD,
SWITZERLAND, TO HONOR
SWISS LIBERTY AROUSED
A FIERCE CONTROVERSY
WHICH ENDED DRAMATICALLY
ON MARCH 6, 1796, WHEN
RAYNAL DIED IN PARIS,
--AND THE OBELISK WAS
DESTROYED BY LIGHTNING
ON THE SAME DAY

PHINEAS P. GAGE
OF CAVENDISH, VT,
SURVIVED AN
EXPLOSION THAT DROVE
A 13-LB. TAMPING IRON
THROUGH HIS BRAIN —
*HE LIVED FOR 12
YEARS WITH A 3½-INCH-
WIDE HOLE IN HIS SKULL!*

THE **CASKET** of **QUEEN ELIZABETH I**
WHILE ON VIEW IN
Whitehall Palace, London,
ON THE EVE OF HER INTERMENT
MYSTERIOUSLY EXPLODED!
THE COFFIN WAS SHATTERED AND HAD
TO BE REPLACED - YET THE QUEEN'S
BODY WAS UNHARMED (Mar. 24, 1603)

JOHN OLSEN of Trumbull, Conn.,
WON TWO NEW CARS IN A ROW IN CONTESTS
SPONSORED BY A CONNECTICUT RADIO STATION ...
THE ODDS AGAINST SUCH A DOUBLE WINNER ARE
16,000,000 TO 1

THE STRANGEST SERIES OF TRAGEDIES IN MARITIME HISTORY !
CAPTAIN EDWARD LADNER, master of the schooner "Dewdrop,"
WAS THROWN OVERBOARD IN A STORM IN 1919, 600 MILES OFF THE
COAST OF BREST, FRANCE, AND HIS BODY WAS NEVER RECOVERED -
HIS FATHER, CAPTAIN EDWARD LADNER, WAS LOST FROM THE
SCHOONER "ARETHUSA" IN 1900, AND HIS GRANDFATHER, CAPTAIN
EDWARD LADNER, VANISHED FROM THE SCHOONER "CAIRNS" IN 1881
--IN STORMS AT THE SAME SPOT !

LIKE FATHER LIKE SON

JOHN HAY

OF HUON ISLAND, TASMANIA,
MARRIED TWICE AND
BECAME THE FATHER OF
10 BOYS AND 12 GIRLS—
HIS NAMESAKE SON, JOHN HAY,
ALSO MARRIED TWICE AND
BECAME THE FATHER OF
10 BOYS AND 12 GIRLS

MARK TWAIN
(1835-1910)
THE FAMED AUTHOR, WAS BORN WHEN HALLEY'S COMET WAS SEEN··· HE PREDICTED HE WOULD DIE WHEN IT REAPPEARED— --AND DIED SHORTLY AFTER IT AGAIN STREAKED ACROSS THE SKY !

THE SWIMMERS WHO WERE SAVED FROM DROWNING BY A WHALE
2 MAORI WOMEN, THE ONLY SURVIVORS WHEN A CANOE SANK IN COOK STRAIT, NEW ZEALAND, WERE SAVED WHEN THEY FOUND FLOATING IN THE WATER **THE CARCASS OF A WHALE**
A HARPOON WAS IMBEDDED IN THE WHALE, AND THE WOMEN PULLED THEM- SELVES ABOARD THE CARCASS BY A LINE TRAILING FROM THE WEAPON --AND FLOATED MORE THAN 80 MILES TO SAFETY (1834)

LORNE GASCHO
OF ELKTON, MICH.,
RECEIVED A POSTCARD
FEB. 3, 1976 THAT HAD BEEN
MAILED TO HIS GRANDFATHER
FROM CHICAGO, ILL.,
ON JAN. 7, 1908 --
THE POSTCARD, ENROUTE
FOR 68 YEARS, WAS DELIVERED
WITHOUT A "POSTAGE DUE"
ALTHOUGH IT CARRIED ONLY
A ONE-CENT STAMP

YUSUKE SHIKAUCHI of Tokyo, Japan, WHO HAD SNEAKED AWAY FROM HIS JOB TO ATTEND A BASEBALL GAME, WON AN AUTOMOBILE RAFFLED OFF AT THE STADIUM-- *AND FOUND HIS PICTURE ON NEWS-PAPER FRONT PAGES*

TWO AUTOMOBILES THAT COLLIDED IN AJAX, ONTARIO, ON A SLIPPERY WINTER DAY WERE OWNED BY MOTORISTS NAMED *SNOW* and *BLIZZARD*

"DANNY YOUNGER"

A PARAKEET OWNED BY
MRS. ELLA HOHENSTEIN,
OF ST. LOUIS, MISSOURI,
WAS RETURNED AFTER
BEING MISSING FOR 4
WEEKS BECAUSE HE KEPT
REPEATING HIS NAME
--*AND IT WAS LISTED IN
THE TELEPHONE BOOK*
THE LISTING ACTUALLY WAS
THAT OF MRS. HOHENSTEIN'S
GRANDSON, AFTER WHOM
THE PARAKEET WAS NAMED

FIRE HOSE SET AFIRE BY COLD WATER!

HIGH PRESSURE CREATED ENOUGH FRICTION HEAT TO SET THE HOSE ON FIRE

F. R. DANIEL, CHIEF ENGINEER
Milwaukee Fire Insurance Rating Bureau

"CLAIMING" A FATHER

WHEN JACK B. MILLER, AN INSURANCE ADJUSTER OF CORAL SPRINGS, FLA., MADE A BUSINESS CALL TO JACK R. MILLER, A SECURITY FIRM OPERATOR OF NORTH MIAMI, FLA., HE LEARNED *HE WAS TALKING WITH THE FATHER HE HADN'T SEEN FOR 31 YEARS*

THE **MOST** *AMAZING* **SHIP RACE IN HISTORY!**
THE **S.S. LUFRA** AND **THE WAGOOLA**
RACED FROM HOBART, TASMANIA, TO
LONDON, ENGLAND--*A DISTANCE OF 11,000
MILES*--AND *FINISHED IN A DEAD HEAT!*
THEY SAILED FROM HOBART ON JULY 26,
1876 AND REACHED LONDON ON
OCT 25th JUST 7 MINUTES APART
--*SO THE 91-DAY RACE WAS
OFFICIALLY PRONOUNCED A TIE*

**SHAKESPEARE'S
"MACBETH"**
SINCE IT FIRST
APPEARED IN 1606,
HAS BROUGHT BAD
LUCK TO MANY IN-
VOLVED WITH IT ...
IN RECENT TIMES,
LAURENCE OLIVIER
WAS ALMOST KILLED
DURING A PERFORM-
ANCE. CHARLTON
HESTON WAS BADLY
INJURED DURING
REHEARSALS. PRES.
LINCOLN READ IT
TO FRIENDS THE
DAY BEFORE HIS
ASSASSINATION

BURTON J. SCHAFFER
OF EASTON, PA.,
WHO MARRIED
LAURA SCHAFFER,
HAS AN AUNT DIANA
WHO MARRIED
JOHN SCHAEFFER,
A COUSIN
FLORENCE WHO
MARRIED SAMUEL
SCHAEFFER, AND
A COUSIN ARLENE
WHO MARRIED
LLEWELLYN SCHAFFER
--AND NONE OF THE
SCHAFFERS OR
SCHAEFFERS WERE
PREVIOUSLY RELATED

MAJOR SUMMERFORD, AN OFFICER IN THE BRITISH ARMY DURING WORLD WAR I, WAS STRUCK **3** TIMES BY LIGHTNING — IN 1918, IN 1924 AND IN 1930. FOUR YEARS AFTER HIS DEATH, LIGHTNING STRUCK AND DESTROYED HIS TOMBSTONE!

A **TURTLE** ON WHICH MELVIN BEACH OF WILLIAMSTON, MICH., ENGRAVED HIS INITIALS IN 1919 WAS RETURNED TO HIM *60 YEARS LATER*

THE *MUSIC* WITH THE MOST TRAGIC SCORE IN OPERATIC HISTORY!

EUGENE MASSOL, TENOR STAR OF THE PARIS OPERA, AT THE PERFORMANCE OF "CHARLES VI" ON FEB. 9, 1849, SANG IN FRENCH THE LINE, "OH, GOD, CRUSH HIM," WITH A FINGER POINTING AT THE VAULTED CEILING *FROM WHICH AT THAT MOMENT A STAGEHAND FELL TO HIS DEATH!*

THE FOLLOWING NIGHT MASSOL POINTED TO AN EMPTY LOGE AS HE SANG THE LINE, BUT A PATRON ENTERED IT *--AND DROPPED DEAD!*

ON THE 3rd NIGHT THE TENOR GESTURED AT THE ORCHESTRA PIT--*AND A MUSICIAN COLLAPSED AND DIED!*

THE OPERA WAS NOT REVIVED UNTIL 1858, WHEN IT WAS TO HONOR EMPEROR NAPOLEON III, BUT ASSASSINS BOMBED THE EMPEROR'S PARTY--*CAUSING 156 CASUALTIES*

The WELL THAT MOURNED COLUMBUS
Palos, Spain

IT SUPPLIED THE WATER FOR THE 3 SHIPS
WITH WHICH COLUMBUS DISCOVERED
THE NEW WORLD — AND DRIED UP
SUDDENLY ON MAY 20, 1506
THE DAY ON WHICH COLUMBUS DIED!

A BOTTLE CONTAINING A NOTE
DESCRIBING THE FATAL INJURY
OF CHUNOSUKE MATSUYAMA AND THE DEATH
OF 44 SHIPMATES ON A HUNT FOR BURIED TREASURE IN 1784 WAS
WASHED ASHORE AT MATSUYAMA'S OWN VILLAGE IN JAPAN 151 YEARS LATER

THE MARINER WHO WAS SAVED FROM DROWNING --*BY THE SEA!* CAPTAIN BRISCO, MASTER OF THE "GRACE HARWAR", WASHED OVERBOARD BY A GIGANTIC WAVE EN ROUTE FROM DELAGOA BAY, E. AFRICA, TO GISBORNE, N.Z., WAS SAVED FROM CERTAIN DEATH WHEN A SECOND WAVE *FLUNG HIM BACK TO HIS ORIGINAL POSITION ON THE SHIP'S BRIDGE* THE VESSEL WAS DISABLED BUT WAS RIGHTED A WEEK LATER AND TOWED TO SAFETY (Dec. 25, 1900)

THE *SHIP* THAT COULD ONLY POSTPONE ITS DOOM!

The "C.S. HOLMES"

BEING SWEPT TOWARD THE ROCKY COAST OF VANCOUVER ISLAND DURING A GALE IN 1909, WAS MIRACULOUSLY SAVED BY A CHANGE IN THE DIRECTION OF THE WIND

41 YEARS LATER ANOTHER GALE WRECKED THE SHIP EXACTLY IN THE SAME POSITION

KAREN POWELL OF GRANDVIEW, WASH., BY COINCIDENCE WAS ASSIGNED BANK ACCOUNT NUMBER 38 9 14999 8 *WHICH IS THE SAME AS HER SOCIAL SECURITY NUMBER 389 14 9998*

THE MAN WHO LOCATED A SOURCE OF WATER 6,000 MILES AWAY !

FATHER ALEXIS MERMET of Saint-Prex, Switzerland, BY HOLDING A PENDULUM OVER A SET OF PLANS IN HIS STUDY *DETERMINED THE EXACT POSITION AND DEPTH OF UNDERGROUND WATER AT THE MONASTERY OF SAN CAMILO, IN POPAYAN, COLOMBIA-*

HE MARKED THE PLANS AT A POINT WHERE HE SAID WATER WOULD BE FOUND AT A DEPTH OF 27 METERS (88 FEET, 9 INCHES) - AND THE UNDERGROUND STREAM WAS FOUND AT THAT EXACT SPOT !

MOREOVER HE CORRECTLY PREDICTED THAT THE WATER WOULD HAVE A FLOW RATE OF 500 LITERS PER MINUTE (1927)

THE CATASTROPHIC FIRE CAUSED BY A SUPERSTITION
A **CONFLAGRATION** THAT BURNED FOR 3 DAYS IN PARIS, FRANCE, IN 1718, WAS STARTED BY A WIDOW WHO LAUNCHED A CANDLE ON THE SEINE RIVER ON A PIECE OF WOOD IN THE BELIEF IT WOULD HELP HER *FIND HER DROWNED SON*
THE CANDLE SET FIRE TO A BOAT, WHICH BURNED A BRIDGE AND 22 BUILDINGS ATOP IT WERE DESTROYED

MRS. SANDY CHARLES of Cuba, New Mexico, GAVE BIRTH TO TWIN DAUGHTERS -- ONE IN CUBA, N.M., AND THE OTHER IN ALBUQUERQUE, N.M. -- *84 MILES AWAY*

THE STRANGE PROPHECY THAT WAS FULFILLED BY A VIOLENT DEATH!

WALTER INGRAM, of London, England, BROUGHT BACK FROM EGYPT IN 1884 THE MUMMIFIED HAND OF AN ANCIENT EGYPTIAN PRINCESS, WHICH WAS FOUND TO BE CLUTCHING A GOLD PLAQUE INSCRIBED:

"WHOEVER TAKES ME AWAY TO A FOREIGN COUNTRY WILL DIE A VIOLENT DEATH AND HIS BONES WILL NEVER BE FOUND!"

4 YEARS LATER INGRAM WAS TRAMPLED TO DEATH BY A ROGUE ELEPHANT NEAR BERBERA, SOMALILAND, AND HIS REMAINS WERE BURIED IN THE DRY BED OF A RIVER BUT AN EXPEDITION SENT TO RECOVER HIS BODY FOUND A FLOOD HAD WASHED IT AWAY

MR. and MRS. L.B. WILLSEY OF SACRAMENTO, CAL., READ AN ADVERTISEMENT DESCRIBING JUST THE KIND OF HOME THEY WANTED AND CALLED THE AGENT—ONLY TO LEARN THAT IT WAS AN AD FOR THEIR OWN HOUSE, PUT ON THE MARKET A MONTH EARLIER

THAT'S IT!

OLIVER ANTHONY OF MEMPHIS, TN, WAS **SHOT BY A ROBBER** WHILE PLAYING GOLF, BUT SURVIVED WHEN *THE BULLET LODGED IN A GOLFBALL INSIDE HIS TROUSER POCKET!*

VISIT THESE RIPLEY'S MUSEUMS

Ripley's Believe It or Not! Museum
7850 Beach Blvd.
Buena Park, California 90620
(714) 522-7932

Ripley's Believe It or Not! Museum
175 Jefferson Street
San Francisco, California 94133
(415) 771-6188

Ripley Memorial Museum/Church of One Tree
492 Sonoma Avenue
Santa Rosa, California 95401
(707) 576-5233

Ripley's Believe It or Not! Museum
19 San Marco Avenue
St. Augustine, Florida 32084
(904) 824-1606

Ripley's Believe It or Not! Museum
202 East Fremont Street
Las Vegas, Nevada 89101
(702) 385-4011

Ripley's Believe It or Not! Museum
202 S.W. Bay Blvd.
Mariner Square
Newport, Oregon 97365
(503) 265-2206

Ripley's Believe It or Not! Museum
901 North Ocean Blvd.
Myrtle Beach, South Carolina 29578
(803) 448-2331

Ripley's Believe It or Not! Museum
800 Parkway
Gatlinburg, Tennessee 37738
(615) 436-5096

Ripley's Belive It or Not! Museum
301 Alamo Plaza (across from the Alamo)
San Antonio, Texas 78205
(512) 224-9299

Ripley's Believe It or Not! Museum
601 East Safari Parkway
Grand Prairie, Texas 75050
(214) 263-2391

Ripley's Believe It or Not! Museum
115 Broadway
Wisconsin Dells, Wisconsin 53965
(608) 254-2184

Ripley's Believe It or Not! Museum
P.O. Box B1
Raptis Plaza, Cavill Mall
Surfer's Paradise, Queensland
Australia 4217
(61) 7-592-0040

Ripley's Believe It or Not! Museum
Units 5 and 6
Ocean Boulevard, South Promenade
Blackpool, Lancashire
England

Ripley's Believe It or Not! Museum
Yong-In Farmland
310, Jeonda-Ri, Pogok-Myon
Yongin-Gun, Kyonggi-do, Korea

Ripley's Believe It or Not! Museum
Aunque Ud. No Lo Crea de Ripley
Londres No. 4
Col. Juarez
C.P. 06600 Mexico, D.F.

Ripley's Believe It or Not! Museum
4960 Clifton Hill
Niagara Falls, Ontario, L2G 3N4
(416) 356-2238

Ripley's Believe It or Not! Museum
Cranberry Village
Cavendish, P.E.I. C0A 1N0
Canada
(902) 963-3444